New Golgotha

Exiled from Pennsyltucky

Christopher Moore

Table of Contents

Nursery Rhymes 2020

Winter of My Discontent

Confederacy of Gangsters

Dark February

Northamptus Imperium

Janus

My Sanity for an Elective

Climbing Koalas

Winter Psalm

My Jericho

New Golgotha

New Nineveh

No Sanctuary

Pennsyltucky Exodus

Modern Iscariot

Devsylvania

Boozton

Yeats on a Sunday

Redneck Jane

Eastern Bangor

The Autism Lash

Preface

After I published my second book of personal poems in July 2019, I thought it would be a long while until I ever publish a third one, or if I would ever publish a third poetry book at all. My third poetry book, *New Golgotha,* continues where *Pennsyltucky Blues* left off, kind of like a volume 2. Unlike *Pennsyltucky Blues* however, it will be entirely comprised of new poems written from my personal collection, so no pre-summer 2019 poem will be in this volume of poetry, since my second book was released in July 2019, the majority of the poems written in post-summer 2019.

New Golgotha got its name out of redemption, personal redemption after years of self-discovery and thought. It is a sacrifice to be made new and how a mindset must be escaped from. With no hope left in this clockwise world of Pennsyltucky, my soul is exiled to New Golgotha. I would like to thank my family and friends for always supporting me in my poetic work no matter what it was. Even if they do not fully understand my poetry, I am happy at the amazement it brings them, thank you all.

Crucified Heart

Here's a nail for each end,
who gives a fuck is blood comes out?
Join me in condemning the wrongs
and we'll all get a piece of this pie.
Make sure the spear goes through the center,
just ignore the cries of repent.
Keep pounding on it like I command,
but just remember, like Lady Macbeth,
there's no blood on my hands.

Summer 2019

Amanda's Eden

Are you sure I can't tempt you
before I start to make you miserable?
Perhaps some of this fruit
will open your eyes to what I done.
This side of paradise is not what it seems.
Once you take a taste from that tree,
this Eden will soon become your Inferno.
Better watch your back,
many serpents hide within the trees.

Summer 2019

Undergrad Tango

Take everything you have learned in history,
now put it in a barrel and burn it.
It is the last week of August,
you have until December 12th to give me a thesis proposal.
Primary sources will be your best friend
for this 25-page paper.
Try not to do anything too common,
no one wants to read an article-length paper
on bread riots or Andersonville.
You're playing with the big boys now.
Fail at your own risk, but if you impress me,
you'll be going places.

Autumn 2019

Tango de Los Muertos

A skeleton dances with a rose in its skull.
He wears a sombrero and despite his skinniness,
accompanies it with a tie.
When the music starts,
his dance begins as he searches around.
His dance partners join him, but not for too long.
He changes partners often
as one after the other falls to the floor with each dance.
He keeps a rose in his teeth
as the dance of the dead endlessly goes on.

Autumn 2019

Pocono Diaspora

Still wandering from an exiled land,
trekking northward
as new obstacles are hurled in my direction.
Things in life I was told would be useful later on
now are completely useless as I have to learn new ways.
Schedules go out of whack
as life's expediencies cause my emotional mind to spin.
I continue to trek through the endless abyss
although the sands of time are far ahead of me.

Autumn 2019

October Night Sky

Primary, primary.
Civil War prisons of the North,
my thesis is out of control.
Sanctuary, sanctuary.
Life if overfilled,
please just give me time
to gather thoughts and emotions.
Thoughts, thoughts.
Still picturing that beautiful smile,
which helps me get by as I rest to await another day.

Autumn 2019

Lucid in the Clouds

Yes, you are possibly having another dream,
welcome to the inner's of your subconscious.
A big oak table floats by as dead relatives have coffee,
you don't know if they ate yet or not, but who cares.
Then a frustrated writer floats by,
clicking away on a typewriter.
One can easily hear the sound of ripping paper
as he bangs his head repeatedly with his fists.
Lastly, you see others circle around a burning building
singing "London Bridge is falling down"
as one lone panicked soul carries bucket after bucket
in hopes everything saved up is not lost forever.

Autumn 2019

Mental Health Drain

Please just take a moment so I can sort this stuff out.
You over there with the work attitude,
I don't need a fucking foreman.
Please shut up with your incessant talking
and leave me the hell alone.
Diary after diary, journal after journal,
how am I suppose to determine what is useful
for this thesis and which is not?
Out of a big thick diary,
only five pages are useful to my research,
how wonderful…
As things circle around and bicker,
the beast is given food to calm in down once more.

Autumn 2019

Snowcapped Babylon

Trekking up a hill as the snow gets deeper with elevation.
A castaway from a messed-up land
begins his long exodus into the mountains.
New lessons are abounded in this strange land,
things he never knew before.
Lessons are learned, mistakes are made,
but our castaway continues onward.
Not knowing is part of the journey
as the snowflakes go on and on.

Autumn 2019

Not-so-Pleasant View

Hey! Don't you dare do that.
I saw you pluck that one pine needle off,
don't deny it!
I don't give a crap
if you don't know what property lines are,
don't let me catch you again.
I have no proof that your particular dog
shit on my lawn even though there are
other dogs in the area,
I'm just going to blame you because I see you often.
Oh, you can't afford a garage?
Well I'm just going to be an ass and build one,
even though I don't really need it.
Welcome to the neighborhood,
now go away.

Autumn 2019

Monty, Monty

He's not the messiah,
he's a very naughty boy.
Oh you mean the People's Front of Judea,
not to be confused with the Judean People's Front.
What do you mean we can't stone him with a bolder?
I didn't expect the kind of Spanish-
NOBODY EXPECTS THE SPANISH INQUISITION!
Our chief weapon is surprise, surprise and fear,
wait, that's two weapons.
Cardinal, fetch-the comfy chair.
My hovercraft is full of eels.
Oh you hear that, bloody peasant,
now we see the injustice inherited in the system.
We want- a shrubbery!
No one throws a stone until I blow this whistle
and I want to make this perfectly clear,
even if they do say Jehovah.
You have no arms,
tis but a scratch.
On second thought, let's not go to Camelot,
tis a silly place.

Autumn 2019

Helen of Dixie

She was not the face that could launch a thousand ships.
Rather, she was one with a face
that could make a man do battle against himself.
A smile that looked so pure,
yet could also cause heartbreak and regret.
Her emerald eyes look down with pleasure
as the war she started rages on.

Autumn 2019

My World

In my world you can't let your emotions out,
less someone thinks you're crazy.
In my world the negatives have become a way of life,
so no use in complaining about it.
In my world you're too stupid to understand,
so best not worry about things.
In my world your problems are small,
who cares and just deal with it.
In my world just go about your life
as you put on happy mask after happy mask.

Autumn 2019

Historian' s Lament

A source here, a source there,
what the fuck do you mean my theory's wrong?
I've been busting my ass since Labor Day on this thing,
where were you when I originally asked for help?
I thought to whole point was to show new perspectives,
did you idiots forget to take your bipolar medication?
The British wrote way too many documents,
do you know how much freaking money I've
had to spend on black ink since September?
Yes, I'm sure British Liberalism will come in handy
when I teach college students
military history of the US Civil War.
Everything you ever been told has been a lie
as you search a long list to find another elective.

Autumn 2019

Teepee in the Sky

Misery, misery, misery.
You people don't understand that I can't do
what I want to do anymore.
No, I don't know what is going on,
I just don't feel myself.
Life has gone downhill anymore.
Can't fix this, can't do that,
everything I want to try doesn't work.
It is time for me to go to the teepee in the sky.

Autumn 2019

Pennsyltucky Winter

All-wheel drive vehicles skid the slippery old 611,
snowflakes come down fast
as ice becomes a burden for old strong oak trees.
Cars outside every home glazed over in ice,
making it difficult for occupants to open them.
The temperature might read 28 degrees,
but I wouldn't trust that number if I were you.
The real feel might be 10 to 15 degrees.
The icy cold rages on outside
as you are trapped inside your multi-story igloo.

Winter 2019-20

How Many Highlighters

Printer ink is out again,
but I still have another document to print for Monday.
There are so many papers in my folders,
both of them are about to break.
What do you mean I can't change my thesis topic,
I'll certainly fail with this current one.
Besides, you said nothing to the others
when they changed their topics just last week.
Another highlighter died,
if I had a dollar for every highlighter I used since August.
Nobody cares about your problems, but don't worry,
a better spring is ahead.

Winter 2019-20

My Civil War

Sucker punches are tossed in the congress inside my mind.
Insults are traded
just because the left side does not agree with the right.
Tasks are left undone
as the nervous system prepares to do battle with itself.
Brain pulses and headaches start
as they clash to see who is right.
As they squabble over stupid things,
the heart begins to race and steam
because it was left unchecked.
When it is all over, it ends up worse than it started.
Both sides are left to think
as the heart goes through it's Reconstruction.

Autumn 2019

Nursery Rhymes 2020

I don't have a six pence
for a pocket full of pies,
if Mary had a little lamb,
it would not be what you'd be thinking of.
Old King Cole would be a fat old bastard
because he should really share his wealth.
This old man would not play eight,
because he got there much too late.
Humpty Dumpty fell off a balcony,
nobody saved him,
but the fall does have 26k views on Facebook,
76k views on Instagram.
Jack and Jill went up the hill
to fetch a pale of vodka,
Jack fell down and did not frown,
but Jill stayed drinking instead of helping.
The Muffin Man has something green
to make his muffins happier.
The little dog laughed like an arrogant snob
and the dish ran for Congress with the spoon.

Winter 2019-20

Winter of My Discontent

Nobody cares about these meaningless problems,
just take each day as it comes and try not to go crazy.
Trying your hardest isn't good enough apparently
because you are right back to were you started
even though you did all that hard work.
Things pile and pile on top of you
as you are given no time to examine them.
Yes, you are miserable, I am miserable,
we all are miserable, join the club.
As another decade dawns,
hopefully the next ten are better than the last.

Winter 2019-20

Confederacy of Gangsters

The south will rise again,
even though I never left the frozen north in my life.
Sure, downtown is not like the slums of New York,
but I am just as much a bad ass gangster as the Bronx.
I don't care if you like it or not,
I need the Monday after Thanksgiving off for hunting.
Let me put my hoodie on
as I drive through cornfields with rap music on too loud.
Just let me finish raising my Confederate Jack
before telling you what the South was really fighting for.
Welcome to the Twilight Zone.

Winter 2019-20

Dark February

Left to wander alone
after being traded in for silver egos.
The judgment of a snowy January
has left me battle-scared in February.
Pelted with stone after stone
as I drag my personal wooden burden between my enemies.
After they were done, my tired soul was left wandering
as it approaches a snowy Babylon to find itself.

Winter 2019-20

Northamptus Imperium

You do what we tell you to,
not what you think is right for us.
You are just a number in our books,
why should we care if you have to wait hours?
If you have a good excuse, we might be compassionate,
that is if we decide it is a good excuse or not.
Comitatu status potissimum[1].

Winter 2019-20

[1]county state above all {Latin}

Janus

Janus, the Roman god for endings and beginnings.
He is looking towards a brighter future
while at the same time, not forgetting the past.
The past, a place of chaos,
indecisive decisions, mistakes,
and things carved in stone that cannot be changed.
The future direction he also looks towards is uncertain.
You may succeed, you may fail,
things might go smoothly or it might be all fucked up.
Unless you move forward however,
you won't know what's ahead.

Winter 2019-20

My Sanity for an Elective

Chalked up last semester as a disaster,
why do I need all of these classes?
Are you sure I need ten more?
South Asia History looks interesting,
but maybe I should stick to what I know.
World History is required,
but the sections are at horrible times.
Of course the one good professor
is only teaching one higher elective,
so much for that idea.
I don't think my mind can stand
a 5 day/week schedule just yet.
My sanity, my sanity,
my sanity for an elective!

Winter 2019-20

Climbing Koalas

Infernos rage in West Aussie
as kangaroos hop for their lives to safety.
Smoke fills the air as the sky turns blood red.
The aired summer heat only makes the flames stronger
as koalas desperately try to find safe trees to hang on.
New South Wales chocks for release among the ashes
while a barren wasteland is all before them.
Panicked residents scatter away from their homes
as the burning monster inches its way down under.
No amount of water on earth can stop its path
as the world pities the continent.

Winter 2019-20

Winter Psalm

Even in eternal darkness there is light.
Things might look bad now,
but brighter days loom ahead.
Hear me oh snow-capped Babylonia,
there will come a day when I will leave
and the luscious promise land of spring will be with me.
I might be exiled to your icy captivity,
but my day will come when I am finally at peace.

Winter 2019-20

My Jericho

Walk once
for your integrity.
Walk twice
for your emotions and mentality.
Walk thrice
for the seasons you were exiled.
Walk fourth
for those who did you wrong.
Walk five-fold
for the days you toiled many years.
Walk sixfold
so your inner demons leave you.
Finally, walk seven
as the walls that block you tumble down.

Winter 2019-20

New Golgotha

The plains of eternal sunset are the only company
for those who lug personal burdens up a hill.
No one there to cure or comfort
as you make that long lonesome heavy climb.
Both to stop or to continue is pointless,
since you have to go through it yourself anyway.
You are left to ponder on your misery
as darkness ascends on New Golgotha.

Winter 2019-20

New Nineveh

Get out the bottles and pour those shots,
if you're not smashed, you're an idiot.
We are holier than thou just by our looks alone.
Bow down like we a goddesses,
don't offer us anything under eight proof.
Dance like there's not care in the world,
we can always repent and do it all over again.
Ignore those who doubt us,
they're just living in their own misery.

Winter 2019-20

No Sanctuary

Misery fills the air like a thick cloud of fog.
Arguments over who is wrong or right
and others finally having enough of it all.
The concerned are of no use to the weary,
escapism can only help so much.
Who can remember joy?
Who can remember happiness?
Full contentment doesn't exist,
so just lie to yourself that everything is fine.

Winter 2019-20

Pennsyltucky Exodus

Nonconformity is my crime,
not becoming a sheep to the slaughter.
Misfit to every group I run into,
whether they like me or not.
No matter what age, what decade,
they're all the same the lot of them.
Trapped in their own delusions
as the outside world ticks along without them.
Do not weep for the exiled,
for their souls are finally free of purgatory.

Winter 2019-20

Modern Iscariot

Et tu Brute?
Do you get joy from crushing me down?
What I have done
to deserve this backstabbing honor?
Was it not your savior who said
judge not less you be judged?
Oh yeah that's right, I forgot.
His words only apply when it suits you.
Enjoy your silver ego as long as it lasts
as you bend your horns to form a halo.

Winter 2019-20

Devsylvania

Everyone can be tempted in the Keystone,
it all depends on what that temptation is.
Maybe someone you don't like should fail,
or perhaps enough fire water will make you forget things.
Turning everyone against you might work
if given the correct opportunity to screw things over.
You might think you have strong will power,
but some higher being lied to you about that.
So before I drive you to complete insanity,
wander a bit in the Keystone of Purgatory.

Winter 2019-20

Boozton

Drink up and get smashed,
clank those wine glasses,
squirt limes into Coronas,
and make those mixed drinks strong.
The more drunk we are, the happier.
Every minor celebration requires it,
you only live once, so make the most of it.
Dace the day and night away
while we're buzzed without a care in the world.

Winter 2019-20

Yeats on a Sunday

Very few words have touched my soul,
but your lyrics are my New Testament.
We all have our Helen of Troys,
in any day or age.
We all have suffered loss,
dreamed of freedom and liberation,
questioned our spirituality and God.
The beast is slouching towards all of us,
as we write to quiet our noisy minds.

Winter 2019-20

Redneck Jane

Redneck Jane loves Fords,
she knows how to shoot a gun,
and also gut a dead deer.
She's got a big Confederate Jack in her room
and as if that weren't enough,
also wears a battle flag bikini
while she's sunbathing by the pool.
Redneck Jane almost always wears hiking boots,
and loves tailgating on trucks drinking beer.
The most shocking thing about Redneck Jane though
is that she lives north of the Mason-Dixon Line.

Winter 2019-20

Eastern Bangor

The sun rises in the Pennsyltucky heartland
as the lock-step population begins their day.
Cars drive down narrow roads
as a cop checks their speed by the cemetery off the road.
Old ladies stop by a restaurant to play cards
and a small library will open in hours for its residents.
Years and decades may come and go,
but this place is locked in its own time warp.
Like from an episode of the Twilight Zone,
everything looks and appears perfect
while its tiny populous say they'll cherish thoughts,
but not for those who have escaped.

Winter 2019-20

The Autism Lash

You are different from others,
therefore we have to replace everything,
because it might not be easy to do.
I know nothing about your emotions,
who knows what mood you'll be in.
I'm going to treat you as if I were walking on glass,
that is until I know what mood you're in today.
Aren't you people suppose to be unsympathetic or something?
I don't know, your head's just messed up.
You looks so normal, I would have never guessed.

Winter 2019-20

North of Eden

You have tasted the forbidden fruit,
nothing is the same as you once knew.
The simpler times are gone
as anger and confusion reign supreme.
Once you think you understood something,
everything just gets fucked up again.
Tread up the long snowy mountain,
for you have failed in paradise.

Winter 2019-20

The Last Temptation

Give away your thoughts,
hand me your heart on a silver platter.
Just give into my beautiful eyes
and the world could be your oyster.
Look into my emerald eyes,
all it will cost is your very soul.
I am your enchanted demon,
with a permanent residency in your subconscious.
You may think I am gone,
but with every second thought you make,
I am freed from your locked history book.

Winter 2019-20

Delaware Baptism

The darkness has ended
and there is light at the end of the tunnel.
You may have had hardships in your past,
but you now have a second chance for rebirth.
Negative energies have clung to your soul
being stoned and crucified in Pennsyltucky
for all of those long many years.
Cleans your soul of the wounds
as the new you has been born.

Winter 2019-20

Ashes of the Soul

Purge yourself of all your doubts
as you prepare to cleans yourself.
Negative thoughts drag you down
and it might be wrongfully said.
Cleans yourself in preparation,
mind, body, and spirit are one.
New exciting beginnings are occurring,
prepare yourself for your rebirth.

Winter 2019-20

Hall of False Goddesses

A row of statues
once worshiped like the golden calf of Israel,
now are memories out of a bad mythology.
Some of them don't mean anything at all,
while others share a deluded past.
No longer as they bowed down to
or given hearts to bite off of silver platters,
those days are long gone.
Memories of stone is all they are
to a mind museum that tries to forget its history.

Winter 2019-20

We Have No Fixation But Caesar

Who cares what was in the past,
all that matters now is we want it solved.
Yes, we think ourselves righteous,
but this is something we can never forgive.
We don't care if you don't see the wrongs,
it is us who are the partial judges.
Skew his very soul,
no forgiveness or redemption.
We have no fixation but Caesar.

Winter 2019-20

Personal Crucifixion

Sometimes I don't give myself enough credit,
I guess that's what makes the nails.
Always thinking about the worst outcome
can sometimes drive me crazy.
Shielding compliments and good deeds
as my thoughts pound the nails into my arms.
I wear a crown of thorns
that block me from hearing the good below.
I think about what put me in this situation
as my redemption is a long way off.

Winter 2019-20

Forbidden Fruit

Congratulations,
you just discovered you've been living a life of ignorance.
How does that make you feel?
Everything you liked now feels stupid,
doesn't it now?
Nothing can calm you down like in the past,
no solution you try will ever help you.
You shouldn't have tried that forbidden fruit,
now there is no turning back.

Winter 2019-20

A Poem to My Readers

So, you made it to the end of the book.
The real question is if you understood the poems.
Some of it might not make sense to you,
but I'm glad you enjoyed it anyway.
This book was a personal redemption of the soul,
a poet's understanding of the crazy world he resides in.
Pennsyltucky to me is both
a geographical location and a mind set.
A mind set of the past and how going beyond that
will be good for this poet's soul as a whole.
I thank you for reading this book
and hope you can exile your own Pennsyltucky.

Spring 2020